IMAGES OF WAR

WAFFEN-SS DUTCH, BELGIAN & DANISH VOLUNTEERS

RARE PHOTOGRAPHS FROM WARTIME ARCHIVES

Ian Baxter

Pen & Sword
MILITARY

First published in Great Britain in 2023 by
PEN & SWORD MILITARY
an imprint of Pen & Sword Books Ltd
Yorkshire – Philadelphia

ISBN 978-1-39908-762-9

A CIP catalogue record for this book is available from the British Library.

Typeset by Concept, Huddersfield, West Yorkshire, HD4 5JL.
Printed and bound in England by CPI Group (UK) Ltd, Croydon CR0 4YY.

FSC www.fsc.org MIX Paper | Supporting responsible forestry FSC® C013604

Pen & Sword Books Limited incorporates the imprints of Atlas, Archaeology, Aviation, Discovery, Family History, Fiction, History, Maritime, Military, Military Classics, Politics, Select, Transport, True Crime, Air World, Frontline Publishing, Leo Cooper, Remember When, Seaforth Publishing, The Praetorian Press, Wharncliffe Local History, Wharncliffe Transport, Wharncliffe True Crime and White Owl.

For a complete list of Pen & Sword titles please contact
PEN & SWORD BOOKS LTD
47 Church Street, Barnsley, South Yorkshire, S70 2AS, England
E-mail: enquiries@pen-and-sword.co.uk
Website: www.pen-and-sword.co.uk
or
PEN & SWORD BOOKS
1950 Lawrence Rd, Havertown, PA 19083, USA
E-mail: uspen-and-sword@casematepublishers.com
Website: www.penandswordbooks.com

Contents

About the Author

Ian Baxter is a military historian who specialises in German twentieth-century military history. He has written more than fifty books including *Poland – The Eighteen Day Victory March, Panzers In North Africa, The Ardennes Offensive, The Western Campaign, The 12th SS Panzer-Division Hitlerjugend, The Waffen-SS on the Western Front, The Waffen-SS on the Eastern Front, The Red Army at Stalingrad, Elite German Forces of World War II, Armoured Warfare, German Tanks of War, Blitzkrieg, Panzer-Divisions at War, Hitler's Panzers, German Armoured Vehicles of World War Two, Last Two Years of the Waffen-SS at War, German Soldier Uniforms and Insignia, German Guns of the Third Reich, Defeat to Retreat: The Last Years of the German Army At War 1943–45, Operation Bagration – the Destruction of Army Group Centre, German Guns of the Third Reich, Rommel and the Afrika Korps, U-Boat War,* and most recently *The Sixth Army and the Road to Stalingrad.* He has written over a hundred articles including 'Last days of Hitler', 'Wolf's Lair', 'The Story of the V1 and V2 Rocket Programme', 'Secret Aircraft of World War Two', 'Rommel at Tobruk', 'Hitler's War With his Generals', 'Secret British Plans to Assassinate Hitler', 'The SS at Arnhem', 'Hitlerjugend', 'Battle of Caen 1944', 'Gebirgsjäger at War', 'Panzer Crews', 'Hitlerjugend Guerrillas', 'Last Battles in the East', 'The Battle of Berlin', and many more. He has also reviewed numerous military studies for publication, supplied thousands of photographs and important documents to various publishers and film production companies worldwide, and lectures to various schools, colleges and universities throughout the United Kingdom and the Southern of Ireland.

Preface

Drawing on a superb collection of rare and often unpublished photographs and text, this book tells the story of how the Dutch, Belgians and Danes volunteered for the Waffen-SS following the German invasion of the Soviet Union, which Hitler called his 'European War'.

It shows how SS Volunteer Legion Netherlands, for instance, grew to become the largest SS unit of the four formations that were created. It operated in Yugoslavia and was sent to Northern Russia. Later in the war the unit was re-designated the 23rd SS Volunteer *Panzergrenadier Division Nederland*.

Fighting alongside the *Nederland* formation was the SS Volunteer *Legion Flandern*, which was a fighting force created mostly from Dutch-speaking recruits from occupied Belgium. This Flemish legion was officially disbanded and later re-formed within the Waffen-SS as the SS Assault Brigade Langemarck (*SS-Sturmbrigade Langemarck*).

Another formation was the SS Volunteer Legion Walloon. It was recruited from French-speaking volunteers from German-occupied Belgium, mainly from Brussels and Wallonia. By 1942 the legion was sent to Russia, later integrated into the Waffen-SS and known as the SS Assault Brigade Wallonia (*SS-Sturmbrigade Wallonien*).

The last unit to be created was the Free Corps Denmark, which was a group of Danish SS recruits put together and sent to the Eastern Front in May 1942. Some 6,000 Danes served in the Free Corps Denmark and within a year the formation was disbanded and re-formed into the Division Nordland known as 'Regiment 24 Danemark'.

This unique book is divided into chapters, each chronicling the history of the individual formations that fought and perished for the Nazis. It shows in graphic detail how these units were forced to withdraw and were required to defend every yard as they fell back towards Berlin in April 1945.

Introduction

A European Crusade

When the German invasion of Russia was unleashed on 22 June 1941, both infantry and panzer divisions wasted no time and soon smashed through the bewildered Soviet forces on every front. The ferocity and effectiveness of the German divisions were so great that some of the Red Army forces they surrounded were gigantic. Groups of up to fifteen Russian divisions were trapped at one time and slowly and systematically annihilated in a hurricane of fire. Many Russian soldiers stood helpless in front of the German war machine, too shocked to take action. Over the weeks to come, German troops continued to chew through enemy positions heading east. It appeared that the war in Russia would be completed before winter set in.

The success of the German invasion of Russia soon brought about pledges of loyalty across Europe. Italy honoured her obligations and declared war against Russia. Romanian soldiers began fighting in the provinces invaded by the Soviet Union a year earlier. Spain confirmed that a Spanish expeditionary force was being recruited to join the fight against communism, and the Hungarian government pledged its allegiance to Germany. In occupied Nazi Europe countries also wanted to assemble a union of forces. In Denmark, Holland and Belgium, Nazi collaborators saw the chance to help crush the 'Bolsheviks' by joining forces with Germany. To them the war against Russia was a head-on conflict between two totalitarian systems that meant life or death. Taking part in the war in the East, they could be proud that their involvement might become the greatest military struggle in the history of mankind. However, this collaboration with Nazi Germany in what was termed a 'crusade' had already seen a number of extreme movements evolve with the rise of Nazism.

When Nazi Germany invaded Holland and Belgium in 1940 no civilian government was installed. Instead a military administration was created, forcing it to intensify its collaboration with Germany. This in turn increased competition between various groups by finding more extreme collaborationists that were willing to side with Germany.

At the time of the German Invasion of the West in 1940, Belgium, for example, already had a number of political parties that were generally sympathetic to the dictatorial and anti-democratic ideals represented by the Nazi regime. In Wallonia and Brussels the largest collaborators were known as the Rexist Party led by Léon Degrelle. Rexists immediately welcomed the German occupation of Belgium, conceitedly supported the occupiers and assisted Wehrmacht and Waffen-SS forces with the repression of territory wherever they could.

Belgium's neighbour Holland also had a number of Nazi movements and these were already established when the Germans invaded the country. One of the largest movements was the *Nationaal-Socialistische Beweging* in the Netherlands or the NSB (National Socialist Movement). Even as early as 1932 this strong movement had its own *Weer Afdeelingen* militia (WA or defence sections). Their role was similar to Nazi Germany's *Sturmabteilung* or SA (Storm Detachment). As in Germany, the WA was motivated by ideological discipline and were committed Nazis. They advocated clear messages tailored to a broad range of people and their problems. They spread propaganda around the country aimed at exploiting people's fear of uncertainty and instability. Many of their messages were purposely directed at the working class and fear of unemployment. Like Germany, Jews and Communists also featured heavily in their propaganda as enemies of the state. However, their movement was short-lived and by the mid-1930s the Dutch government had prohibited them.

However, it would not be until five years later in May 1940 when the WA was re-established following the country's occupation by Germany. By then the Dutch government and the royal family had escaped to England, leaving the German Dr Seyss-Inquart to be appointed Reich Commissioner for the occupied Netherlands. With the country now under Nazi occupation, Hitler personally made a public appeal in writing calling for the reintegration of the Netherlands into the 'Germanic' community. Seyss-Inquart immediately began establishing policies to prepare the state structure and Dutch population for National Socialist ideology. The Nazi vision they wanted to create was of a 'new Europe' led by Germany in which the countries could be ultimately incorporated into the Reich after its victory in the war. However, Seyss-Inquart was conscious that the majority of the Dutch people would not agree with his vision, so he decided to adjust his approach of rule in order not to raise any unwanted disturbances by the Dutch people. He was also aware that the local Fascist and Nazi movements in the Netherlands, particularly the NSB led by Anton Mussert, were generally hated by the Dutch people. Instead, he formulated propaganda and fear in the country by telling the population of the growing menace of the Soviet Union and its aims to destroy Western civilization. He also decided to appoint and indoctrinate a number of NSB members and other Germanophiles to senior posts like secretaries-general and mayors.

Although the Dutch movement did not have much ideological influence on the administration of the country, with its assistance the Germans were able to exert much tighter control over Dutch citizens than in military-occupied countries as with the French government in Vichy. The nature of the Dutch system meant that without military administration the country was able to undertake various Nazi-sponsored policies, especially persecution of the Jews. With the general absence of any Wehrmacht control over the running of the country, it also allowed civilians and the agencies operated by *SS-Reichsführer* Himmler's SS more freedom. This in turn made it easier for Himmler to undertake an extensive recruitment programme for the Waffen-SS in the country.

In Demark, its occupation by Germany in 1940 saw the National Socialist Workers' Party of Denmark or the DNSAP wanting to install a Nazi government. However, due to the policy of co-operation with the legitimate Danish government, it was deemed better to wait until Germany had won the war. Yet in spite of this, the DNSAP continued its pro-Nazi movement, even establishing its own Storm Troopers, the SA or *Storm Afdeling*, whose normal service dress was a brown shirt with black breeches and black-topped boots, a black tie and a black brassard with a white swastika.

Chapter One

Belgium

Flandern, Wallonien and *Langemarck*

In order to increase and further German support, the Belgian Walloon and Nazi collaborator Léon Degrelle and his Rexist party attempted to bring it closer to the German occupation authorities. When Germany invaded the Soviet Union in June 1941 Degrelle embraced the attack and gave the Germans their full support. He even announced to the authorities the idea of raising a military unit that would perhaps support the Germans both in the occupation of Belgium and on the battlefields of Russia. In Degrelle's mind he wanted to collaborate militarily in order to increase the importance of the movement and destroy any political competition to his regime. At the same time, the Flemish National League and a rival totalitarian party in Flanders also announced its intention to form a military unit in support of the Nazi regime with a mixture of Walloon and Flemish volunteers into a 'Flemish Legion' where they could fight 'arm in arm' in the Soviet Union against their 'feared enemy'. Though the support was welcomed by the German authorities, the Nazis considered the Walloons an inferior race to the Flemish, and wanted the Walloon and Flemish volunteers segregated into different units.

The Flemish Legion was a collaborationist military formation recruited among Dutch-speaking volunteers from German-occupied Belgium and mainly from Flanders. It was formed in July 1941 and comprised approximately 1,200 recruits who were given nationally independent status as the SS Volunteer Legion Flanders or *SS-Freiwilligen Legion Flandern*. Following its training in Dębica, Poland, the Flemish volunteers were transferred to Arys camp in East Prussia and put through the last part of their training before being sent to the Eastern Front.

On 6 November the *Legion Flandern* received orders for transport to the Leningrad Front, where it was engaged in security operations behind the River Volkhov front near Lake Ladoga in the north and Novgorod near Lake Ilmen in the south. Losses for the legion were terrible, with little shelter and extreme arctic conditions coupled with continuous attacks from Red Army units.

By the end of January 1942, what remained of the legion arrived at Podbjerjezhje and fought a series of battles north-west from the River Volkhov between Novgorod and Chudovo. After weeks of defensive fighting the *Flandern* was almost destroyed. What remained of the legion continued fighting against a number of Soviet attacks and by April it became part of the 18th Army's operations to cut off and encircle the 2nd Shock Army. The Shock Army was annihilated and of what remained, some 32,000 Russians were taken prisoner. The legion fought with distinction.

In July the legion was moved to Osjewa where its units were re-equipped. It was made operational again in August when it fought hard on the Leningrad Front. When winter set in the front once again stagnated, but the legion was better prepared for winter operations. Between January and April units of the *Flandern* continued fighting around Leningrad. Once again heavy battles and losses meant that its units were again pulled out of the front and transferred back to Dębica. It was then moved to Milovitz near Prague to be reorganized.

Fighting alongside the *Flandern* were Walloon legions under the command of Degrelle. At the same time as the *Flandern* was raised, Degrelle was given permission to raise a combat formation and requested prominent Rexists to join in support of the invasion of Russia. A couple of weeks later a Walloon Legion was raised and out of the 860 volunteers, 730 were Rexists. Unlike equivalent Flemish and Dutch units, the Walloon Legion was established within the Wehrmacht because the Walloons were not regarded as 'Germanic' enough to be allowed into the Waffen-SS. Another problem was that a number of the non-Rexist recruits were unwilling to swear personal allegiance to Adolf Hitler, while others were classed as medically unfit.

Training of the Walloon Legion was undertaken in Meseritz, Germany and it was officially designated as Infantry Battalion 373 or *Infanterie Bataillon* 373. Apart from extensive military training and various manoeuvres, each recruit was imbued with Nazi propaganda and anti-communist teachings. When training was completed in November 1941, the Walloon Legion was deployed on security operations in the rear areas of the Eastern Front. In January and February 1942 the legion became embroiled in heavy fighting in and around Gromowaja-Balka and soon distinguished itself on the battlefield with Degrelle in command. Though the battle had cost the battalion 65 dead and 110 wounded, they had forced Russian troops to withdraw from the area. On 13 March thirty-seven Walloon volunteers were decorated with the Iron Cross 2nd Class for their bravery in the field.

Due to the severe losses sustained in Gromowaja-Balka between March and early May, the legion was assigned as a reserve unit to recuperate. Within weeks as the German southern summer offensive in the Ukraine grew in momentum, the Walloons were marched east from Brakowka towards Shukri, where they were put under the direct control of the 97th *Jager* Division. In early July they were then ordered to march south towards the Caucasus where they crossed the River Don at Mrlekovskia and reached the Kuban at Armavir by the last week of August. The

Walloons then attacked the village of Prusskaia, pushing back strong Red Army formations.

Over the next days and weeks the Walloons fought well, utilizing the support of Wehrmacht units to drive the enemy from their positions. By September, with success in the Caucasus looming and the Battle of Stalingrad under way on the River Volga, the Belgian units were limited to reconnaissance operations. The legion did see heavy fighting at Hromova-Balka near Donetsk in the early winter. Here the Walloons suffered a high casualty rate, both from combat and disease, but continued fighting throughout the rest of 1942. However, with such a high loss rate many more volunteers were required to bolster the dwindling ranks. Degrelle became desperate and began a recruitment campaign which included lowering the age requirement for volunteers. As a result a number of Rex's Youth were taken including paramilitary recruits. Himmler supported a propaganda campaign across Belgium for volunteers. He was well aware that the German war machine required more men to face the Red Army, and the occupied countries would be able to provide this resource. As a gesture the *Reichsführer* declared the Walloons to be a Germanic race, which soon saw their units incorporated into the Waffen-SS. The Walloon Legion was then reorganized into a brigade-sized unit of 2,000 men and was bestowed the title *5.SS Freiwilligen Sturmbrigade Wallonien*.

The new *Sturmbrigade* was then sent to a training camp near Meseritz. It comprised some 1,600 veterans of the legion and the Belgian army, along with 400 new recruits drafted across Belgium. The men consisted of craftsmen, young workers, civic leaders, diplomats, industrialists and ex-Belgian army soldiers. Commanding these new volunteers was Lucien Lippert, a 29-year-old military graduate from Brussels who was given the rank of *SS-Obersturmbannführer*. His second-in-command was none other than *SS-Hauptsturmführer* Léon Degrelle, who was given one of the infantry companies to command.

While training the brigade was visited by Himmler on 16 and 24 June 1943, and due to the conditions at the training camp and lack of military equipment the *Reichsführer* decided to transfer the men to the better-equipped training camp at Wildflecken. As the brigade transferred to the new camp on 3 July 1943, the unit was finally upgraded to the *SS-Sturmbrigade Wallonien*. It now boasted three companies, two heavy weapons companies, a replacement company, five heavy weapons platoons, one motorized transport column, a motorcycle platoon, and an assault gun battery was being considered. The anti-tank troops were sent to a special training camp at Arys, East Prussia with the infantry gun crews being sent to Breslau-Lissa. Engineer soldiers were transferred to the SS Combat Engineer School at Dresden. All the infantry remained at Wildflecken where they were rejoined by the heavy weapons section in October. They then continued their training together.

As further battles on the Eastern Front intensified, the *Wallonien* was called upon to assist in reinforcing the 5th SS Panzer-Division *Wiking* on the Lower Dnieper in the Ukraine. Here the *Wiking* Division was fighting to prevent large Soviet forces encircling them. On the night of 19/20 November the *Wallonien* arrived at a rail siding at Korsun in six troop trains. Here the Belgian legions were placed under the *Wiking* commander *SS-Gruppenführer* Herbert-Otto Grille. The *Sturmbrigade* was then ordered to move its units along the River Olshanka and undertake a series of reconnaissance patrols in December 1943. In thick snow and freezing arctic temperatures the men were repeatedly attacked in the surrounding forests, this later becoming known as the battle of the Korsun-Cherkasy pocket. Losses in the pocket were huge and by February 1944 the *Sturmbrigade* had suffered 70 per cent casualties. During weeks of fighting, two large Soviet army fronts tried to eradicate the pocket. The encircled German units frantically attempted a break-out in coordination with a relief attempt by other German forces. However, massive losses were incurred and by the end of the engagement the effective strength of the unit had been reduced from 2,000 to 632. The Walloon volunteers were once again withdrawn from front-line operations and transferred back to their training camp in Wildflecken. Days later they were then moved and transferred to Beverloo Camp, the training ground of the new premier 12th Waffen-SS Panzer-Division *Hitlerjugend*. Following their move to Beverloo, remnants of the Walloons were paraded in Charleroi on 1 April to counter any claims made by the enemy that they had been completely destroyed. During the parade seventy-five of the volunteers were decorated with the Iron Cross. The unit was later sent to Brussels and paraded through the streets, borrowing vehicles from the *Hitlerjugend*.

Later in April 1944, the Walloons were sent back to Wildflecken to reorganize. The brigade comprised a total of 1,188 soldiers of all ranks. Weeks later in July the Walloons were transferred back to the Eastern Front on the coast of Finland along strong defensive positions under *SS-Freiwilligen Sturmbrigade Langemarck*.

The *Langemarck* brigade had been raised in May 1943 and comprised a motley collection of volunteers from Flanders, a few Finnish volunteers and Flemish veterans transferred from the ranks of the 2nd *SS-Das Reich* Division. In fact, the disbanded Flemish Legion SS Volunteer Legion Flanders or *SS-Freiwilligen Legion Flandern* was re-formed within the Waffen-SS as the SS Assault Brigade *Langemarck*.

The Flemish formation was about the same size as the *Walloon* brigade, but its organization differed. While the basic components comprised two battalions, the first of these was a grenadier battalion with 1st–3rd rifle companies and a 4th heavy company equipped with MG 34 and MG 42 machine guns and mortars. The second heavy battalion comprised anti-tank, infantry howitzers, light and heavy anti-aircraft guns and armoured tracked assault guns. The brigade was completely motorized.

Training of the brigade was completed in December 1943, and it was then transferred to the River Dnieper fighting alongside Wehrmacht formations in Army Group South. Within days of its arrival it saw a number of battles against units of the 2nd Ukrainian Front which was defending a line between Kiev and Cherkassy. In mid-January during the Russian winter offensive it fought alongside *Das Reich* in the Molotchky-Lubar area. It then linked with units of the *SS-Leibstandarte* and for a few weeks it saw extensive fighting at Shepetivka and then at Bilohorodka.

On 19 February *Langemarck*, following vicious fighting, handed over its positions around the towns of Zherenivka and Stetkovzie to Wehrmacht formations and moved to join units of the premier Waffen-SS divisions *Leibstandarte* and *Das Reich*. Over the next week *Langemarck* fought hard against strongly-held Red Army positions including fighting off attacks on the brigade's headquarters at Bilohorodka. Surrounding the headquarters were well-placed flak companies and strongly-armed Wehrmacht units with a string of heavy MG 34 and 42 machine-gunners. However, in spite of the resistance, Russian attacks began to grind down German and Flemish positions, pushing them further west. Huge casualties were inflicted on the Flemish troops and by April 1944 after more than five months of bitter fighting, from the 2,000 troops that had entered the battlefield only 400 of all ranks remained. Their remnants were then forced to withdraw via Romania and Hungary and halted at Jasło in Eastern Poland.

On 3 May it arrived at a training camp at Knovíz in Bohemia. Here at the camp the brigade regrouped, rebuilt, re-equipped and reorganized. By the end of June there was a recorded total of 1,751 soldiers of all ranks. *Langemarck* was then ordered on 12 July to transfer its rebuilt units to the front line in northern Estonia to begin what later became known as the battle of the European SS. These Flemish units were part of Army Group North and were required to defend the city of Narva against the overwhelming might of the Soviet 2nd Baltic, 3rd Baltic and Leningrad fronts. Emplaced in and around the city was Felix Steiner's III SS Panzer Corps, which consisted of SS European volunteers of Dutch, Flemish, Walloon, Norwegian, Swedish, Danish and German forces. The veteran East Prussian 11th Infantry Division had been added, including the undertrained and under-armed 4th and 6th Estonian Border Guards regiments. However, despite this force, the Red Army had a 4:1 superiority both in manpower and equipment.

Over the next couple of weeks a series of heavy attacks saw a large section of soldiers withdraw from Narva and fall back on the Tannenberg Line. In total, some 22,250 troops were deployed in twenty-five Estonian and twenty-four German, Dutch, Danish, Flemish, Italian, Norwegian and Walloon battalions. Over the days and weeks that followed, the Germans continued to hold their lines despite incurring 10,000 casualties. Although the Tannenberg Line remained intact in a number of places, Estonia was lost. Those troops that remained in various pockets of resistance in Estonia were mainly attributed to the fact that the Soviets had halted in a number of areas as they were now preparing a new assault known as the Baltic offensive. This would see the last German formations finally flushed out of Estonia and those divisions that had withdrawn into Latvia would be cut off.

Through August the Walloons fought a number of enemy contacts as they withdrew against the massive Soviet onslaught. Although III SS Panzer Corps attempted to screen the European SS from these heavy attacks, the cost to the units was enormous. Losses among the Walloons were huge and as a result the destroyed battalion was withdrawn from the front. Those Belgians that were left standing were all decorated with the Iron Cross.

On 20 September 1944 it was decided that a new 28 *SS-Freiwilligen* Grenadier Division *Wallonien* would be raised in honour of the decimated one. From the remnants of the last battalion, they were gathered together with airmen, unemployed sailors and raw recruits. The division was a motley collection of soldiers and was a shadow of its former self. It was officially upgraded in October, but despite its upgrading, the actual strength remained that of a reinforced brigade of around 8,000 soldiers.

The division was sent along with a French force from the Legion of French Volunteers Against Bolshevism and a Spanish contingent of the Blue Division. They were formed into a *Kampfgruppe* and sent to the region near Stargard and Stettin in Pomerania, joining the XXIX Panzer Corps, part of Felix Steiner's XI SS Panzer Army.

Weeks later the *Wallonien* was sent to relieve Wehrmacht troops encircled at Arnswalde in Pomerania. On 15 February the offensive was launched between the Madu See and the Plone See which saw some successes against strong Russian forces. However, despite the XI Panzer Army causing heavy casualties, the offensive stalled with *Wallonien* units suffering substantial losses. As a result, it was compelled to withdraw from enemy contact while Russian forces chased them at speed, thundering to the Oder near Stettin. Over the coming weeks heavy fighting ensued throughout central Pomerania with the *Wallonien* and *Langemarck* units fighting side by side. Eventually, under heavy pressure from overwhelming Russian strength, both Belgian forces were reluctantly pushed back across the river in early April 1945.

After the final Soviet offensive on 20 April 1945, the Belgians tried their best to hold on to their bombed and blasted positions as long as possible until they were finally swept aside by a powerful Soviet thrust bound for Berlin. In spite of a number of fierce counterattacks, it was realized that all hope of sustaining themselves on the battlefield was lost. On the point of total destruction, Degrelle ordered his troops to make it to Lübeck, where they eventually surrendered to British troops. As for Degrelle, he decided to try to evade capture with his bodyguard and drove to Denmark. He then took a Heinkel He 111 aircraft and flew it from Norway to Spain, where he spent the rest of his life in exile.

A recruiting poster for the Waffen-SS and the *Flandern* Legion. It depicts a soldier dressed in a Waffen-SS uniform. He is flanked by a sculpture of an armoured medieval knight and the silhouettes of historical buildings. A heraldic lion, the emblem of the *Flandern* Waffen-SS, can be seen in the background.

Three photographs showing the training of new *Flandern* recruits into the Waffen-SS. In early August 1941 the recruits were sent to the Dębica training camp in Poland. Suitable candidates were sent to a number of specialist training schools, some to the signals school in Nuremberg and others to the pioneer combat engineers' school in Breslau. *(NA)*

Three flags at full mast fluttering in the wind at one of the *Flandern* training schools. The flag on the left is the standard SS flag, the one in the middle is the Nazi national flag and the one on the right is the lion emblem of the *Flandern* Legion. *(NA)*

Aside from military training, the recruits were required to exercise thoroughly. One form of physical training that bonded the men as a team was football. Here they are preparing to play against their fellow comrades with the Nazi national flag on the edge of the football pitch. *(NA)*

The 'Flemish Lions' as they were nicknamed can be seen here in a series of images during a marching ceremony to the main central train station in Antwerp for departure to Germany. The photographs show the soldiers passing through the main streets of the city followed by a drum and fife section, including regimental bandsmen and trumpeters, playing to the jubilation of their commanders as they stand in honour saluting them as the procession passes. Flag-bearers with the lion emblem of the *Flandern* Legion can be clearly identified. *(NA)*

S

Etam

GANTERIE ELEGANTE

CIGARES

A Flemish soldier can be seen here with his motorcycle on board a flatbed railway car destined for the front line. One of the hazards of travelling by motorcycle, especially in northern Russia, was the lack of good-quality roads for vehicles. Riding through the great expanses of trees set in tangled undergrowth would prove a perilous undertaking and the casualty rate among motorcyclists was inevitably high. *(NA)*

Flandern Legions parade before their departure to Germany and then to the Eastern Front. Flowers are attached to their tunics by family, loved ones and supporters. *(NA)*

Men from a signal corps can be seen here standing next to a radio set. The portable radio set, *Tornisterfunkgerät* b1 (Torn. Fu. b1 (S/E) or 'pack radio', was widely used on the Eastern Front. They were carried in two parts by the radiomen on specially-designed backpack frames. *(NA)*

Two photographs showing an *SS-Obertruppführer* with his horse. In the Flemish Legion a number of commanders in the field including troop leaders like this soldier travelled by horseback from one part of the front to another and to command their troops in the field. *(NA)*

A soldier is seen here either repairing or making minor adjustments to the engine of a Volkswagen *Kübelwagen*. *(NA)*

Commanders in the field stand next to a vehicle while a soldier tries to deduce the location of their enemy through a pair of binoculars. *(NA)*

(**Above**) Waffen-SS *Wallonien* recruiting poster for the Walloon Legion. Posters like this were also designed to attract recruits to Léon Degrelle's *SS-Sturmbrigade Wallonien*: *'Venez avec nous!'* ('Come with us!')

(**Opposite**) Fourteen photographs taken in sequence showing a Walloon PaK crew during a training exercise. They are manhandling a 7.5cm PaK 40 from its shelter into position for firing during a training exercise. The 7.5cm PaK 40 became the workhorse of infantry anti-tank units during operations on the Eastern Front. It was the most widely-used anti-tank gun by both premier Waffen-SS divisions and foreign volunteers. It was capable of penetrating the frontal armour of most Russian tanks and was deadly to all of them from the flanks and rear. If properly used by a well-trained crew, this PaK gun could be employed to supplement divisional field artillery. (*NA*)

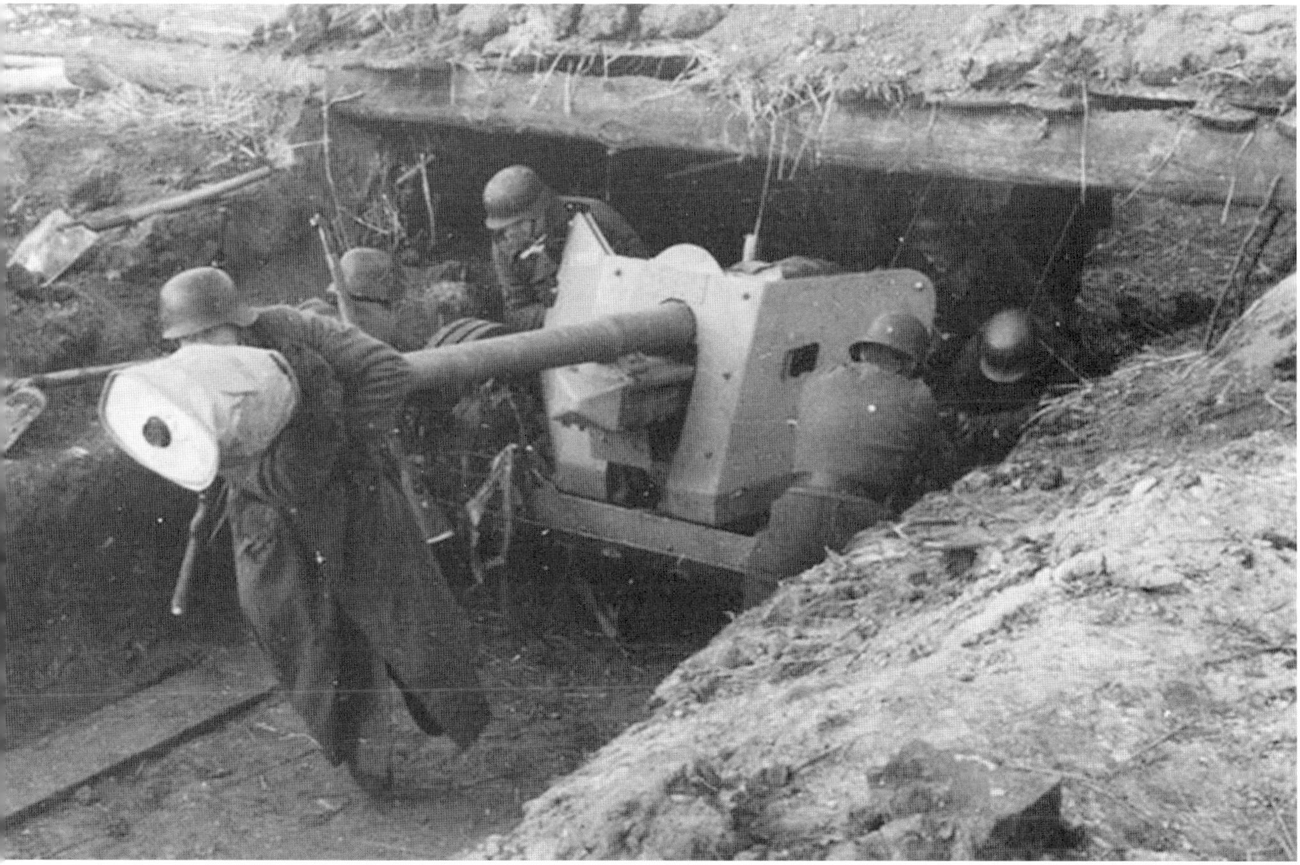

Five photographs taken in sequence showing *Wallonien truppen* along the front lines. In early November 1941 the *Wallonien* Legion arrived in Dnepropetrovsk, Ukraine. During the days and weeks that followed the soldiers dug in and undertook a number of security missions. *(NA)*

A series of photographs showing Walloon mortar troops during an enemy action. The well dug-in 8cm sGrW 34 mortar is being prepared for firing. It was very common for infantry, especially during long intensive periods of action, to fire their mortar either from trenches or dug-in positions where the mortar crew could be protected from enemy fire. Note how the crew duck for cover to avoid the back-blast as the projectile leaves the gun tube. Two of the ammunition-handlers or loaders can be seen holding the tripod to keep it steady and accurate when firing. *(NA)*

FlaK troops belonging to the SS Volunteer *Sturmbrigade Wallonien* preparing their weapon against a probable enemy target. One of the crewmen can be seen trying to locate the enemy through a pair of binoculars and will then shout orders to his gunner and loader. *(NA)*

Soldiers on the Narva Front in 1944 during a pause in defensive fighting can be seen here on a bridge. Both soldiers wear the familiar Waffen-SS reversible parka that was worn extensively by premier SS divisions during the war on the Eastern Front. *(NA)*

Two photographs taken in sequence showing Léon Degrelle speaking to troops at Charleroi, Hainaut, Belgium on 1 April 1944 during a decoration ceremony. Note Josef Dietrich in the background. That day Degrelle paraded through the streets of Charleroi in a vehicle borrowed from the 12th SS *Hitlerjugend* Division, then billeted at the Beverloo Barracks, Belgium.

An anti-Semitic recruitment poster for the *SS-Sturmbrigade Langemarck*.

The first of three photographs taken in sequence showing *Langemarck* volunteers training with a FlaK gun. The majority of the training was undertaken at Milowitz, while engineers were instructed at Pikowitz. The grenadier battalion consisted of 12 × 2cm FlaK guns. *(NA)*

A PaK crew training with a 7.5cm PaK 40. The battalion comprised 9 × 7.5cm PaK 40 guns. During training crews learned the art of teaming anti-tank guns with tanks in both defensive and offensive actions. Quite frequently, tanks would advance to contact and then attempt to draw the enemy into an anti-tank screen, which was commonly called a 'PaK Front'. *(NA)*

During training these troops, more than likely part of a PaK crew, can be seen with a *Selbstfahrlafetten-Zielfernrohr* S.F.14. This device was primarily used for observation and reconnaissance purposes. It measured angles of azimuth, angles of sight, elevation, height of shell burst and establishing a safety area for advancing troops to move forward. The second photograph shows the use of the *Selbstfahrlafetten-Zielfernrohr* S.F. 14 and the S.F. 14Z scissor periscope. Although the periscope, commonly known as 'donkey ears', was able to estimate ranges, it provided a narrow field of vision. *(NA)*

Infantrymen are training here and can be seen shuffling along the ground while their commander oversees the manoeuvre. This type of movement was commonly used by soldiers in the field in order to conceal their advance towards a position. *(NA)*

The first of two photographs showing a FlaK crew training with an 8.8cm FlaK gun. These guns were the mainstay of the Luftwaffe, Wehrmacht and the Waffen-SS anti-aircraft units. Initially these FlaK guns were designed solely for the anti-aircraft role, but after use in a ground-support role in Spain during the Spanish Civil War, direct sights and shields were fitted, turning it into a dual-purpose weapon. In the order of battle in July 1943, the battalion included 9 × 8.8cm FlaK guns. *(NA)*

During training a machine-gunner can be seen here looking through the sight of a heavy MG 34 on the sustained-fire mount. Each infantry battalion contained an MG company, which fielded some eight MG 34 heavy machine guns on the sustained-fire mount. An MG company often had tremendous staying power against enemy infantry and machine-gunners were continuously deploying their weapons in the most advantageous defensive and offensive positions. To obtain the sustained-fire capability necessary for this role, the heavy MG 34 machine-gun positions were normally provided with three or four spare barrels. Groups of light machine guns had only one spare barrel. *(NA)*

Out on the battlefield and a soldier can be seen here mounted on a horse. The brigade was transferred to the Eastern Front in December 1943 where it fought defensive actions west of the River Dnieper in the Ukraine. *(NA)*

Two photographs showing a soldier demonstrating how to use a *Panzerfaust* during winter operations on the Eastern Front in 1944. During the last year of the war the *Panzerfaust* was used extensively to combat Russian armour. It was a hand-held rocket-propelled grenade, which was effective at a range of about 90ft. This weapon became very effective against enemy tanks during the last months of the war and as a result of their effectiveness on the battlefield some tank units often waited for infantry support before advancing in order to minimize the risk of being knocked out. The high kill rate of the *Panzerfaust* is, however, attributed mainly to the lack of German anti-tank guns late in the war and also the terrain where the fighting took place. *(NA)*

A Ukrainian boy assisting two soldiers with a horse during winter operations. It was common for civilians to help the Germans with various menial tasks such as feeding and saddling up horses, clearing roads and digging trenches. The locals often undertook these tasks purely in return for food. *(NA)*

Soldiers can be seen here with their commanding officer in one of many shelters erected along the German front during operations in the Ukraine. These shelters were called *Halbgruppenunterstand* (group and half-group living bunkers). These would become essential for the men if they were to survive the ceaseless artillery and terrible freezing weather conditions. *(NA)*

Three photographs taken in sequence during an enemy action. The crew of this well-concealed 7.5cm PaK 40 is about to fire against an enemy target during operations in 1944. Note the protective shield for the gunner on the left next to the breech-block. It was designed to prevent him being injured in the heat of battle when the gun tube was recoiled. *(NA)*

1

Three photographs taken in sequence showing rocket artillery or *Nebelwerfers*. These deadly weapons fired 2.5kg shells from a tube-mounted rocket-launcher. The projectiles could fire to a maximum range of 7,000 metres. When fired the projectiles screamed through the air, causing the enemy to become unnerved by the noise. These fearsome weapons that caused extensive carnage to the enemy lines served in independent rocket-launcher battalions and in regiments and brigades. *(NA)*

A PaK soldier poses for the camera during winter operations in Russia in 1944. *(NA)*

Two photographs, one showing twin brothers posing for the camera clad in their winter whites. The other image shows the brothers laughing with their comrades. Both are serving in the PaK 5th Company in January 1944. *(NA)*

Another two photographs showing the twins, this time loading a shell into the breech-block of a 7.5cm PaK 40. *(NA)*

Four photographs showing one of the 2cm FlaK 38 cannon of the brigade's 8th Company during operations in March 1944. Note two of the images showing the crew with the two-wheeled trailer *Sonderanhänger* 51 ('Trailer 51'). Set-up of the gun into a position could be accomplished by dropping the gun off its two-wheeled trailer and levelling it using hand cranks. The effect was a triangular base that allowed fire in all directions. *(NA)*

Four photographs taken in sequence showing 8.8cm FlaK guns engaging what appears to be a Russian ground target. The sequence shows the crew working intensely at servicing their weapon. Note the gun's 102 trailer nearby so the crew could limber up and move it quickly to another position. Although the gun could be fired from its trailer, most gunners fired dismounted. A well-trained crew could dismount a gun and be prepared to fire in twenty seconds. It could then take them roughly one minute to remount the gun on its trailer. *(NA)*

Two commanding officers converse in a Ukrainian village during winter operations in 1944. *(NA)*

Chapter Two

The Netherlands

Nederland

The Netherlands was one of the largest of the countries in the West to enlist volunteers, with a high proportion of these recruits enrolled into the Waffen-SS. For them, they wanted to be part of a military elite and involved in a crusade to save Western culture and defeat Bolshevism.

On 25 May 1940, a new formation was established and known as the SS *Westland* Regiment. The volunteers comprised Dutch and Flemish-speaking Belgians and were under the command of SS Hilmar Wäckerle. In fact, Wäckerle had been the first concentration camp commander at Dachau. During his command at the camp he was regarded as a callous and evil man who regularly had inmates executed for the slightest infringement of camp rules. He was later criminally charged with various acts of cruelty and left his post a few months later. When he was given the post of commander of the SS *Westland* Regiment he wasted no time in indoctrinating his new recruits by ordering them to follow blind and absolute obedience. At the Freimann barracks in Munich the Dutch volunteers not only had to learn about enemies of the state but were also given an in-depth indoctrination in SS philosophy and racial superiority. Wäckerle assumed that these ideological teachings would produce men who ardently believed in the new Aryan order. However, the majority of the recruits were neither racist nor had any real belief in an Aryan order. Many had joined the Waffen-SS in order to protect their country from Bolshevism and felt duty-bound to join arms with the Nazis and defend the West. However, in the eyes of Himmler, the foreign Waffen-SS recruits were mere cannon-fodder that existed simply to protect Germanic civilization from the 'Bolshevik hordes'.

To further enthuse the new Dutch recruits, on 9 June 1940 *SS-Obergruppenfuhrer* Gottlob Berger, who was chief of the main office responsible for recruiting for the SS, was sent in person to give the young men encouragement. Berger realized that the Waffen-SS quotas for enlistment had been lower than expected and was determined that these foreign recruitments would bolster the numbers. By doing this he organized the training and equipping of the men. He knew that Himmler needed as many divisions as possible, even if that meant some Waffen-SS formations would be of lower quality. Initial efforts at integrating the recruits from Western Europe and Scandinavia were far from adequate, with insufficient training and the appointment of officers and non-commissioned officers that were drawn from the ranks of the new recruits. In order to remedy this problem, Berger was determined to train the recruits to a physical standard where they could also be ideologically indoctrinated. In his eyes this was an attempt to address the problems of some commanders relating to the quality of the new recruits and their ability to be integrated into units composed mostly of Reich Germans. As a result Berger established a special camp at Senheim in occupied Alsace where recruits were sent for training. A number of various foreign volunteers were brought to the camp including *Volksdeutsche* (ethnic Germans from outside the Reich), Norwegians, Danes, Flemings and Dutch. Berger also created a network of offices throughout German-occupied Europe to ensure the welfare of the families of such recruits. He knew that by doing this he could influence the local communities to support Waffen-SS recruiting and prepare potential volunteers for indoctrination.

By the end of 1940, *SS-Westland* had become the basis for the formation of the fourth Waffen-SS division, *SS-Division Wiking*. The division was formed around three motorized infantry regiments, *Germania*, *Westland* and *Nordland*, with the addition of an artillery regiment.

Months later in April 1941, a third SS regiment was created known as *Nordwest*. It comprised a mixture of what Himmler called racially 'Germanic' volunteers of Flemish, Danish and Dutch men. The commander put in charge of this new Waffen-SS formation of foreign volunteers was *SS-Standartenführer* Otto Reich. The formation was titled the *SS-Freiwilligen Standarte Nordwest* or SS-Volunteer Standard Northwest. Within four months of its creation there were some 2,500 volunteers including 108 Danes, 805 Flemings and 1,400 Dutch. Intensive training was first undertaken in Hamburg and then the recruits were sent to Radom in Poland. It was here that the formation was split in two, with the Dutch volunteers transferred to Krakow while their Flemish counterparts remained in Radom. Initially it was suggested that the *Nordwest* should be employed as a security force in North-West Europe, but when the Germans invaded the Soviet Union in June 1941, it was agreed that the European Waffen-SS should fight on the Eastern Front. Himmler then instructed that the European SS units be transferred into their respective national legions and that the *Nordwest* formation be disbanded. In the eyes of Himmler a new Germanic SS order of European SS Legions would fight on the 'blood-soaked fields of Russia' alongside their 'German brothers'.

On 10 July 1941 *Reichskommissar* Seyss-Inquart officially announced the formation, with the full support of the German authorities, of a Dutch SS legion. It was named the *Freiwilligen Legion Niederlande* and its commander was General Hendrik

Alexander Seyffardt, a Nazi sympathizer and a nationalist. Being a fierce anti-communist, he saw the potential of a Dutch legion that would fight alongside the German war machine in Russia and 'destroy Bolshevism forever'. Almost immediately a large recruitment campaign was undertaken in which all members of the NSB were invited to enlist. Many members of the NSB were recruited including 1,400 Dutch volunteers from the disbanded *Nordwest* Regiment. Some Flemish recruits also joined, including immigrants from the Netherlands East Indies. The formation was the size of a reinforced infantry battalion, with five motorized companies. In mid-October 1941 the Dutch Legion was transferred to Arys in East Prussia to begin an intensive training programme.

Training of the recruits was harsh and their commanders unsympathetic. This led to disgruntled men followed by defections. The unit's commander Seyffardt then learned that his Dutch formation was merely to be a combat unit of the Waffen-SS without any national independence. As a result he resigned, but was made honorary commander-in-chief in order to try to maintain morale among the men. His command was taken over by German *SS-Oberführer* Otto Reich.

In November 1941, the legion was ordered to the Eastern Front near Leningrad under the overall command of Army Group North Rear Area. However, it would not be until January 1942 that the Dutch Legion was ready for combat service. In total there were some 3,000 men organized into three infantry battalions with four companies. The legion was transferred by sea from Danzig in Poland to Libau in Latvia, and then by train it was steamed to the River Volkhov from south-east of Leningrad, near Lake Ladoga in the north and Lake Ilmen in the south. Here the Dutch force undertook rear security actions in freezing arctic temperatures, while Russian forces planned to halt the German advance on Leningrad by building up strong divisions that made up the Volkhov Front.

Along a string of trenches reminiscent of the First World War, soldiers of the *Freiwilligen Legion Niederlande* clad in a variety of early winter white garments over their standard field dress began fighting on the west bank of the Volkhov near Selo-Gora. Over a period of days and weeks men of the Dutch Legion fought a series of counterattacks against strong Red Army forces. The ferocity of the Russian attack was immense and without respite, with the offensive continuing until the end of February 1942. However, German counterattacks were strong and fierce, inflicting considerable numbers of casualties on the enemy. As Red Army units were pounded by heavy artillery and tanks, the Dutch soldiers were tasked with mopping-up lightly opposed pockets where Red Army units had been severely mauled. For weeks the Dutch infantry and their 13th and 14th Anti-Tank companies fought continuously, managing to neutralize a number of enemy areas that were contested by every yard of ground. In fact, the legion had done so well that it was recognized for its gallantry in the official Wehrmacht press release on 4 March 1942.

As fighting continued to escalate in the spring thaw, the legion's commander Otto Reich was temporarily replaced by *SS-Obersturmbannführer* Arved Theuermann. Under Theuermann's command, he watched and manoeuvred his legions as they continued fighting heavily in the Selo-Gora region. They fought successfully and by June the units were relieved from the front line. For their conduct on the battlefield they were awarded 32 Iron Crosses 1st Class and 158 2nd Class.

In June the Dutch Legion was subordinated to the 2.SS-Infantry Brigade under the command of *SS-Brigadeführer* Gottfried Klingemann. On 15 July *SS-Brigadeführer* Josef Fitzthum became the Dutch commander. He ordered that once areas in the Volkhov region were secured, his men were to be moved and undertake security patrols along the Leningrad–Novgorod railway line supported by the 285th Security Division. In July the legion was ordered to take part in the siege of Leningrad and over the coming weeks it fought a series of assaults to repel Soviet counterattacks. The unit was then ordered to take part in an offensive named Operation *NORDLICHT* ('Northern Light'), but it was called off in order to repel a new Russian attack known as the Sinyavino offensive. After about a month of heavy fighting the legion was moved south near Lake Ladoga, where it took up positions to hold off strong Soviet attacks.

In early September a *Kampfgruppe* was formed and named after the legion's commander Fitzthum. It comprised Dutch, Norwegian and the 19th and 20th Latvian battalions. For days and weeks *Kampfgruppe* Fitzthum was engaged in heavy battles that saw it repel a succession of Soviet attacks but suffer high casualty rates.

Although the legions had shown considerable skill and endurance on the battlefield against the Russians, by late 1942 a sense of futility and gloom was gripping the German front lines in northern Russia. Thousands of soldiers had been killed and many units found themselves substantially in the same position that they were in spring. From the River Volkhov to the Gulf of Finland the front was reminiscent of the First World War, with a string of trenches and shell holes in which gains and losses could be measured only in yards.

In Leningrad, despite the prevailing conditions and the daily shelling, the city gradually regained strength and became a strong fortress capable of withstanding a further year and a half of siege and every enemy attempt to destroy it. Costly as this defence was, it managed to pin down huge sections of the German Army Group North that were desperately needed elsewhere to plug the crumbling front.

In January 1943 the Russians unleashed their winter offensive, which was greeted with trepidation by the Germans. From their relatively inactive front they watched anxiously as the Russians began increasing their attacks. *Kampfgruppe* Fitzthum was particularly hard pressed to deal with the overwhelming enemy strength, and losses quickly mounted in spite of tenacious fighting by the Waffen-SS legions.

Yet despite the setbacks on the Eastern Front, it was this endurance coupled with skill and tenacity in Russia that led to Hitler's decision to expand the Waffen-SS.

Initially he had been against expanding, but by late 1942 events on the Eastern Front had forced him to give up his earlier optimism and face facts that the war would be a long-drawn-out battle of attrition.

During this period of expansion the Waffen-SS for the first time had to resort to the large-scale conscription of foreign recruits. Thousands of youths who met SS standards were drafted from the work camps of the Reich Labour Service. Nordic volunteers and *Volksdeutsche* – people of Germanic descent from countries in Eastern Europe – helped to dilute the so-called pure Nordic stock with foreign blood. Over the next two years this expansion saw the final Waffen-SS order of battle of thirty-eight divisions, though the later divisions never approached the proper level of manpower. Foreign soldiers prominently manned many of these divisions. Only about twelve of them were true elite divisions, most being formed late in the war and divisions in name only, often poorly equipped.

As for the Dutch legions, they were to be absorbed into new formations as full members of the Waffen-SS. This then saw the creation of the III *Panzer-SS-Korps* constructed around the *5.SS-Panzer Division Wiking*, which also included a number of foreign conscripts. Himmler was determined to create a new European order of Waffen-SS volunteers including Danish and Dutch formations. The divisional title proposed was *Nordland*, but the Dutch nationalist leader Mussert opposed the name as it sounded like a Scandinavian title. Instead, Himmler agreed to form an entirely Dutch SS component of soldiers which would fight alongside *Nordland*. In March 1943, the 11.*SS.Freiwilligen-Panzgrenadier-Division Nordland* was created by merging the four Germanic legions, units from the *5.SS.Division Wiking* and a large group of new West European recruits. A month later, the Dutch Legion was redesignated as *SS-Freiwilligen Panzergrenadier Brigade Nederland*. Following the redesignation a large recruitment programme was undertaken to enlist more soldiers into *Nederland*. By the summer of 1943 some 5,000 soldiers were part of the brigade. It comprised three battalion regiments and was organized around two armoured infantry regiments, an artillery regiment, a reconnaissance company, an engineer company and an anti-tank company supported by *Sturmgeschütz* IIIs. The brigade was commanded by *SS-Oberführer* Jürgen Wagner and the formation was assigned to *III.SS Panzer-Korps*.

Training of the brigade was undertaken in Zagreb, Croatia, where another 1,500 reinforcements strengthened the formation. From its training facility the brigade was moved to undertake security actions against Tito's communist partisans. It was then transferred back to the Eastern Front.

Nederland arrived on the Oranienbaum front at the end of December 1943. It recorded some 9,342 soldiers of all ranks. The brigade still lacked anti-aircraft and artillery guns, and the reconnaissance company comprised an under-strength motley collection of motor vehicles. Here along the front which was composed of a number of trenches and defensive positions, the Germans and their Foreign Legion counterparts were to try to prevent the Red Army from moving westwards towards the borders of the Baltic States of Estonia, Latvia and Lithuania. It was here that German troops were ordered to 'stand and fight' and wage an unprecedented battle of attrition.

By mid-January 1944 the Red Army had lifted the siege of Leningrad, had gone onto the offensive and was slowly but inexorably driving the German forces westwards towards the Baltic States of Estonia and Latvia. It was in this sector that most of the Waffen-SS volunteer divisions were deployed to try to stem the Soviet drive. The main Waffen-SS force in the area was *SS.Grupppenführer* Felix Steiner's III *Germanic Panzer-Korps*, the *11.SS.Freiwilligen-Division Nordland* and *SS.Freiwilligen Brigade Nederland*. In addition to these volunteer divisions were the *15.* and *19.Waffengrenadier* divisions from Estonia, as well as the Flemish *Langemarck* Brigade and the Walloon *Sturmbrigade Wallonien*. Although regarded as second-rate SS divisions, these troops were formidable opponents, but despite their best efforts nothing could mask the fact that they were dwarfed by the superiority of the Red Army. It was estimated that the Russians had some 2 million men alone on the northern front. For the SS volunteer soldier facing the might of the enemy, the outcome was almost certain death.

During the second half of January the Russians had ploughed their way westwards and by the end of the month had reached German fortified positions at the city of Narva. This German defensive line with hundreds of dug-in artillery positions and machine-gun nests ran from the city south along the banks of the River Narva to the shores of Lake Peipus and down to Polotsk, north-west of Vitebsk. On the west bank of the River Narva SS units had constructed heavily-defended emplacements. Here the soldiers of *Nordland Nederland* were determined to stand firm and fight in what became known as 'the Battle of the European SS'.

The main brunt of the Soviet attack was to fall on Steiner's *SS.Korps* positioned east of Narva. On 3 February, the Soviet assault was finally unleashed and a bloody battle ensued. Almost immediately a Russian armoured group quickly penetrated the German line and established a bridgehead on the western bank of the Narva. The *Nordland*'s *Panzer Abteilung*, named *Hermann von Salza* and commanded by *SS-Obersturmbannführer* Paul-Albert Kausch assisted by Tiger ace *Leutnant* Otto Carius and a platoon of four Tigers crashed into action. Quickly eliminating the Soviet armour, the Panzers and Tigers then began supporting the *SS-Grenadiers* as they cleared out the Soviet infantry. Although the crisis was temporarily averted in the centre, further north Red Army forces successfully established a bridgehead near the village of Siivertsi.

To the south of the city of Narva, in the zone defended by an ad-hoc army *Abteilung* named *Narwa*, Russian soldiers crossed the river and threatened to cut off Steiner's *SS Korps* and two Wehrmacht units. The *502.Schwere Panzer-Abteilung* was moved into the threatened area and quickly stabilized the German line. To strengthen the German defences, the newly-formed Estonian *20.Waffengrenadier-Division der SS (Estnische Nr. 1)* was rushed into the line and attached to Steiner's *Korps*. Steiner threw the division into battle on 20 February against the Siivertsi bridgehead. By 24 February the Russian spearheads had reached the main rail line supplying the Narva area and threatened to encircle Steiner's *Korps* to the north. Despite heavy resistance, the Red Army pushed forward using heavy artillery and armour to smash through the German defences. *Armee-Abteilung Narwa* rushed forces south to halt the Soviet advance. A battalion from the *Nordland*'s *26.SS-Panzergrenadier Regiment Norge* was also brought south to help bolster the disintegrating line.

Despite sustaining massive losses and being repelled a number of times, the Russians persistently attacked all across the Narva line. Determined more than ever to crush the German defences, Russian forces undertook a heavy assault in the Lilienbach area. This was defended by men of the *Nederland*'s *49.SS-Freiwilligen-Panzergrenadier-Regiment de Ruyter* commanded by *SS-Obersturmbannführer* Hans Collani, a Finnish veteran of the *Wiking* Division. Following a huge artillery duel between the *Nederland* and the Red Army attackers, the assault disintegrated into fierce hand-to-hand fighting. After several hours of ferocious combat, the Russians withdrew with huge losses. *De Ruyter* had held the line and the Soviets decided to shift the focus of their attack elsewhere.

Over the following weeks, *Nederland* was subjected to almost constant artillery and aerial bombardments. On the night of 6/7 March, the Red Air Force made a huge bombing raid on Narva, flattening the city. This was followed by a sustained artillery attack from hundreds of artillery pieces. The *Nederland*'s *48.SS-Freiwilligen-Panzergrenadier-Regiment General Seyffardt*, commanded by *SS-Standartenführer* Wolfgang Jörchel and positioned to the south of *Denmark*, was attacked and forced from their positions. What followed was a ferocious counterattack with SS troops fighting in hand-to-hand combat.

All along the German defensive line fierce fighting continued throughout March and April, with the Russians gaining little ground against the tenacious German defenders. During this period the Red Army increased the intensity of their bombardments and began a series of infantry attacks. The main thrust of the Soviet attack shifted against positions at Lilienbach, which was held by the Dutch volunteer regiment *De Ruiter*. Once again the SS held firm and fought to the last drop of blood. However, with huge losses in men and equipment, it soon became apparent that they would no longer be able to hold their position for any appreciable length of time.

Despite the resilience displayed by the Germans at Narva, by mid-June the German bridgehead on the east bank opposite the city had been greatly reduced and its position was becoming more precarious with each successive day. As a consequence, it was decided to finally pull back to a new defensive position further west to the so-called Tannenberg Line or *Tannenbergstellung* located on a series of hills to the west of Narva.

All along the Narva front both Waffen-SS and Wehrmacht soldiers fought shoulder-to-shoulder trying to stem the enemy onslaught. In spite of Hitler's orders to stand or die, a general withdrawal was made to the Tannenberg Line. As Steiner's *Korps* retreated, the *Nederland* was tasked with covering the withdrawal, with the *General Seyffardt* Regiment and the artillery battalion being the last units to withdraw across the battered Narva bridge. The regiment itself soon became pinned down in bitter fighting and attacked by both air and ground forces. Slowly and systematically the regiment was bled white, and as the last few remnants of the force tried to escape the slaughter, they too were annihilated.

By the summer of 1944 men of the *Nederland* were fully aware that the Red Army had only been delayed, not halted. On 23 July, Steiner ordered a withdrawal of his forces to the Tannenberg Line. *Nederland* then became exposed to heavy air attack the following day and sustained a considerable number of casualties. Remnants of the regiment were then ordered to be re-formed at Schlochau. By September, Léon Degrelle's *Kampfgruppe* from SS Brigade *Wallonien* was placed under the command of *Nederland*. The unit was then transferred to positions in the area near Gumi-Wolmar in mid-October where it was tasked with holding a defensive line against strong Soviet forces in the Baltics. This became known as the Kurland pocket, where some thirty-three German divisions of Army Group North became trapped.

On 26 January 1945, the brigade received orders to evacuate the pocket by sea and urgently ordered troops to the Swinemünde-Stettin area to defend the Oder Line. On 10 February, the brigade was redesignated the 23rd *SS Volunteer Panzer-grenadier Division Nederland*, with a strength of 1,000 men.

A Waffen-SS propaganda recruitment poster. The soldier depicted here is *SS-Obersturmbannführer* Klemens Behler of the 23rd SS Division *Nederland*.

A Dutch Waffen-SS propaganda recruitment poster. It reads: 'Who is the real Dutchman?'

Two photographs showing commanding officers during an official visit to the *Nederland* Legion. (NA)

Three photographs taken in sequence showing troops collecting rations from the rear of a horse-drawn wagon during operations in northern Russia. Note that two of the soldiers are wearing mosquito-proof head nets. Mosquitoes were a major problem for the soldiers in Russia, especially during the spring and summer periods. *(NA)*

A typical log cabin constructed in the forests of northern Russia during the summer of 1942. During this period the Dutch Legion was operating on the Volkhov Front. *(NA)*

Three photographs showing troops utilizing their Zeltbahn shelter quarters as tents during a pause in the fighting in the summer of 1942. *(NA)*

A soldier appears to be pumping water into a tin bucket from the tank on the rear of a support truck. He wears the distinctive Waffen-SS summer camouflage smock and a mosquito net. *(NA)*

Two photographs of a legionaire armed with the 98k bolt-action rifle and wearing the Waffen-SS summer camouflage smock on patrol along the Volkhov Front in 1942. (*NA*)

Armed with the standard infantryman's Karabiner 98k bolt-action rifle, this legionaire is at a forward observation post during operations in the summer of 1942. *(NA)*

A series of photographs showing *Nederland* troops during decoration ceremonies. During operations on the Volkhov Front alone, Dutch volunteers were awarded 32 Iron Crosses 1st Class and 158 2nd Class for their battlefield actions between February and June 1942. Many more were decorated for their bravery fighting on the Oranienbaum Front, Narva, holding positions doggedly along the *Tannenbergstellung* and at Kurland. *(NA)*

Two photographs showing *Nederland* commanding officers visiting a war cemetery. *(NA)*

Two soldiers on patrol during summer operations in 1942. Once sweeps had been completed along the Volkhov Front, the Dutch were moved to patrol the Leningrad–Novgorod railway line. *(NA)*

A soldier is seen here holding an ammunition box in front of his *Scharführer* or squad leader. *(NA)*

A *Scharführer* holding a pair of binoculars can be seen here with an SS-Man or trooper armed with a 98k bolt-action rifle. They appear to be on a patrol. *(NA)*

Soldiers concealed in long grass, more than likely during a training exercise, along with a light MG 34 machine-gunner. In open terrain the MG 34 machine-gun squad would normally use their sustained-fire mount to protect the flanks of advancing rifle companies.

Sometimes, MG crews had to operate forward with the rifle platoons and in light machine-gun roles with bipods only and advance very quickly, as in this photo. They were still able to sometimes take advantage of the situation and revert to a heavy machine-gun role. *(NA)*

Clad in his Waffen-SS anorak grey-side-out, this soldier appears to be patrolling a forward observation post armed with his infantryman's rifle. *(NA)*

Soldiers inside a log cabin shelter during operations in 1943. Much of the front remained stagnant in the north, especially during the winter periods. As a result, the men often tried to make the shelters as homely as possible, furnishing them with photographs and other home comforts. *(NA)*

A very young *Rottenführer* or section leader poses for the camera. (*NA*)

A close-up photo of an infantryman wearing the Waffen-SS anorak grey-side-out. The anorak was intended for mobile personnel, predominantly for operations on the Eastern Front. *(NA)*

Two photographs showing a *Sturmführer* ('Storm Leader') inside an Sd.Kfz.251 command half-track armed with an MG 42 machine gun for local defence. *(NA)*

A photograph showing an independent tank battalion maintenance team undertaking repairs to a panzer. Much was owed to the specialist maintenance teams that kept the armour in fighting condition. Note that the engine has been removed for repair. *(NA)*

Troops halt during their march in order to deduce the whereabouts of their enemy. Note two of the troops wearing mosquito nets attached to their M1938 field caps.

Winter-clad soldiers along a defensive line towards the end of 1944. Note the whitewashed *Panzerfaust* lying in the snow in preparation for use against advancing Russian tanks. *(NA)*

During operations in the winter of 1944, losses in the legion were high. Here soldiers wearing their winter whites hastily move an injured comrade to safety on a sled. *(NA)*

Chapter Three

Denmark

Free Corps Denmark

In 1939 Denmark signed a treaty of non-aggression with the Nazi government. However, on 9 April 1940 Hitler revoked this treaty when he ordered the military occupation of Denmark under the pretext of protecting the Danes from British invasion. Eager to neutralize any threat from the Danish people, Germany gave Denmark diplomatic and economic support. What grew from this support was a policy of collaboration and this included the expansion of the National Socialist Workers' Party of Denmark (DNSAP).

When Germany invaded Russia on 22 June 1941, the Nazis asked Denmark to form a military corps to fight in an alliance with the German Reich against the growing threat of Bolshevism. A week later on 29 June 1941, the Danish Nazi Party newspaper *Fædrelandet* (*The Fatherland*) proclaimed the creation of the Free Corps Denmark. It called upon officers and soldiers of the Royal Danish Army to join arms against Russia. There was also a recruitment programme designed purely to persuade right-wing nationalists that were eager to see the destruction of communism. The volunteers were encouraged to enlist on the grounds that the war against Russia was a crusade to 'protect Europe against Bolshevism'. As a result, the so-called *Frikorps Danmark* was established. Almost half the Danish volunteers were members of the DNSAP and 1,000 of the first recruits were sent to Langenhorn barracks in Hamburg for basic training in late July 1941.

By mid-September the Danish volunteers were considered ready for combat and sent to Owińka in Poland. Initially the Danes were used for security operations in Army Group North. During the winter of 1941 and early 1942 the front in northern Russia stagnated. It was not until May 1942 that men of the *Frikorps Danmark* were sent to Demyansk, south of Novgorod. However, in less than three months the corps lost some 350 soldiers either killed or wounded. It was then pulled out of the front line and ordered back to Denmark for recuperation and re-equipment, but upon the corps' return home in August 1942, the men were met with hostility from the civilian population. Yet despite the animosity it did not deter the DNSAP from continuing to generate propaganda across the country to support what they called the 'corps' crusade' in the East.

On 13 November 1942 the corps was redeployed to Jelgava in Latvia to undertake anti-partisan operations. However, as the military situation deteriorated, the Danes were sent to the front in December where the corps engaged in a series of heavy battles around Velikiye Luki supporting the German 1st SS Infantry Brigade. The fighting in the region became known as the Battle of Velikiye Luki, also called the Velikiye Luki offensive. It was a Russian winter offensive with the objective of liberating the Russian city of Velikiye Luki. Strong Red Army forces encircled the city on 27 November 1942, but were unable to make further progress against well-dug-in German units further west. As further fighting intensified and the Russians closed around Velikiye Luki, the German garrison inside the city was ordered to hold out for a relief force and put up a concerted defence. What followed bore similarities to what was happening at Stalingrad in the south. By mid-January 1943 the garrison finally surrendered. Losses in the area were huge and the Danish force was once again pulled out of the front after making hardly any military impact on the situation.

In March 1943, what was left of the corps was sent to Grafenwöhr near Nuremberg before being disbanded on 6 June. Most of the soldiers were transferred to *Regiment 24 Danmark* in the 11th *SS-Freiwilligen-Panzergrenadier-Division Nordland*. The regiment comprised three battalions and formed part of III *SS-Panzer Korps*. Initially *Regiment 24 Danmark* was sent to Glina, Hrastovica, Petrinja and Sisak in Yugoslavia to undertake security measures against growing partisan activity in the region. However, as the military situation deteriorated further on the Eastern Front, *Regiment 24 Danmark* was redeployed over Christmas 1943 and sent west of Leningrad. Over the coming weeks and months fighting intensified in Army Group North and Soviet forces began driving German and SS European legions westwards into Estonia. German forces continued to fanatically hold on to their positions along the Baltic coast. Along the frontier of Estonia they had been defending Narva and well-fortified positions outside the city for months in anticipation of the Soviet advance.

In fact on 23 March 1944, Hitler declared Narva a fortress and the city to be held at all costs, but with ammunition running low and casualties rising, the defence of Narva seemed an impossible task. However, by early April the Germans were reprieved from the clutches of the Red Army as the spring thaw arrived, bringing an end to large-scale attacks. During April and May the front stagnated and allowed both sides to rest and regroup. By the end of May as the ground began to dry the Russians were preparing its southern flank for an all-out attack against the town of Dolgaja Niva, held by the *Nordland*'s *Danmark* Regiment.

On 7 June 1944, the Russians unleashed a powerful attack against the Narva Front. The entire Thirteenth Air Army of the Red Air Force took to the skies against minimal Luftwaffe opposition. A massive combined air and ground attack was then unleashed against *Nordland*'s positions, and over the next four days the SS desperately tried to hold their shattered defences against wave upon wave of strong infantry attacks. Despite futile attempts to hold back the Russian drive, by 12 June they had managed to break through the Danish lines and occupy the strongpoint known as 'Post Sunshine'. Only scattered forces now blocked the Russian route to the bridges over the River Narva. One of these forces was the remnant of *7.Company Danmark* commanded by *SS-Scharführer* Egon Christoffersen. Although heavily outnumbered, Christoffersen was not deterred by the strength of his opponent and quickly ordered his small force forward to meet the advancing Russians. For the next several hours both sides fought a series of savage close-quarter battles before Christoffersen's men finally recaptured 'Post Sunshine' and restored the line. Christoffersen was awarded the Knight's Cross for his actions. Although the fighting continued for another two weeks, the Red Army made no progress against the remnants of *Danmark*.

In spite of the resilience displayed by the Germans at Narva, by mid-June the German bridgehead on the east bank opposite the city had been greatly reduced and its position was becoming more precarious with each passing day. As a consequence it was decided to finally pull back to a new defensive position further west, to the so-called Tannenberg Line or *Tannenbergstellung* located on a series of hills to the west of Narva.

All along the Narva front both Waffen-SS and Wehrmacht soldiers fought shoulder-to-shoulder trying to stem the enemy onslaught. In spite of Hitler's orders to stand or die, a general withdrawal was made to the Tannenberg Line. As Steiner's *Korps* retreated, the *Nederland* was tasked with covering the withdrawal, with the *General Seyffardt* Regiment and the artillery battalion to be the last units to withdraw across the battered Narva bridge. The regiment itself soon became pinned down in bitter fighting and attacked by both air and ground forces. Slowly and systematically the regiment was bled white and as the last few remnants of the force tried to escape the slaughter, they too were annihilated.

Elsewhere on the front, the situation had also deteriorated. A massive Soviet push from the north had finally forced Danish volunteers across the River Narva. Reluctantly the units were compelled to withdraw their forces westwards, fighting for every foot of ground as they retreated across a scarred battlefield.

The Battle of Narva was finally over. While the Russians claimed victory, the Germans and their Waffen-SS Europeans had in fact delayed the enemy advance for a number of months and inflicted terrible damage on their forces. Although the first half of 1944 had been a period of disasters for the German army on the Eastern Front, Hitler had good reason to be pleased with the performance of his Waffen-SS. They had shown their courage in the face of overwhelming strength and stood firm against almost impossible odds. Narva was one battle that stood as an example of the SS making sacrifice after sacrifice, often holding the line to allow other units to escape.

From 27 July 1944, the Danes with *Nordland* fought alongside the 20th *Waffen-SS Grenadier Division of the SS* (1st Estonian) with parts of the *Grossdeutschland* Division. Following heavy fighting and overwhelming enemy strength, its units retreated into what was known as the Kurland Pocket. From late October to December 1944, *Nordland* remained in the pocket and to escape decimation in January 1945 it was ordered to the Baltic port of Libau, where it was evacuated by sea.

During the last months of the war German forces continued to recede across a scarred and devastated wasteland. On both the Western and Eastern Fronts, the last agonizing moments of the war were played out. While British and American troops were poised to cross the River Rhine, in the East the terrifying advance of the Red Army was bearing down on the River Oder, pushing back the last remnants of Hitler's exhausted units. The resistance of his once mighty armies was now collapsing amid the ruins of the Reich. Most of the so-called Waffen-SS crack divisions were still embroiled in heavy fighting in Hungary and were unable to be released in order to plug the massive gaps in the German front lines in the East. This left the northern and central sectors of the Eastern Front to East and West European SS volunteers. Many of the volunteers, spurred on by the worrying prospect of the Russian occupation of Europe and certain death if captured, were determined to defend to the bitter end and try to hold back the Red Army advance.

Over the next days and weeks German troops, together with what was left of the European SS, were pushed further west towards the Reich capital of Berlin. It would be here that the soldiers would be required to fight their last battles.

A recruitment poster reading 'Denmark: Fight against Bolshevism'. It shows *SS-Rottenführer* Sven Borg of the *SS-Panzergrenadier* Regiment 24 *Danmark* holding an MP 38/40 machine pistol in front of a Danish Viking.

Danish flag used by the 'Free Corps Denmark'. This photo was probably taken at the Langenhorn Barracks in Hamburg for basic training in late July 1941. *(NA)*

Two photographs showing troops putting up recruitment posters for Slavs living in the Croatian Republic of Herceg-Bosna. These soldiers more than likely belong to Regiment 24 Danmark which was sent to Glina, Hrastovica, Petrinja and Sisak in Yugoslavia to undertake security measures against growing partisan activity in the region.

HRVATI HERCEG-BOSNE!
HRVATI!

(**Above left**) A portrait image of *SS-Obersturmbannführer* Christian Peder Kryssing who became the commander of the Danes on 19 July 1941. By August 1941, Kryssing had built up a battalion strength of 1,000 men with many of its members being drafted from the ranks of the defeated Danish army. However, due to differences of opinion with *SS-Reichsführer* Heinrich Himmler, he was discharged as commander in 1942.

(**Above centre**) *SS-Obersturmbannführer* Christian von Schalburg replaced Kryssing on 1 March 1942. One of the main reasons for Schalburg's posting was his political dependability and enthusiasm to offer his corps ideological training. He also enjoyed good relations with his subordinates, something lacking in his predecessor. However, weeks later during the *Frikorps Danmark* offensive on the Eastern Front he stepped on a Russian mine on 2 June 1942 and was later killed by shrapnel from an enemy shell.

(**Above right**) *SS-Obersturmbannführer* Knud Børge Martinsen. Martinsen was temporary commander between von Schalburg's death and *SS-Obersturmbannführer* Hans Albert von Lettow-Vorbeck's appointment. However, when von Lettow-Vorbeck was killed only two days after his appointment, Martinsen then took over as commander and remained as commander until the disbandment of the *Frikorps Danmark* on 20 May 1943.

(**Right**) *SS-Obersturmbannführer* Hans Albert von Lettow-Vorbeck took command of the *Frikorps Danmark* on 9 June and two days later was killed in action during intense fighting near Dubowitz.

Danish volunteers during a training exercise at the Langenhorn Barracks in Hamburg. The recruits are being put through strenuous exercises on an assault course. *(NA)*

A recruit belonging to the Regiment 24 Danmark can be seen during a training exercise with his German issue Karabiner 98k bolt-action rifle. *(NA)*

Two photographs taken in sequence showing Danish recruits being lectured by one of their trainers in the summer of 1941. Due to the number of nationalists that volunteered into the *Frikorps Danmark*, commanders could easily indoctrinate them into hating Bolshevism and conjure up increased anti-Semitism. (*NA*)

An *SS-Rottenführer* on the left, an *SS-Scharführer* in the middle and an *SS-Sturmführer* standing on the right during a passing-out ceremony at the training barracks in the summer of 1941. Danish soldiers can be seen standing to attention behind the three men armed with their standard German-issue Karabiner 98k bolt-action rifles. *(NA)*

Seen here is a trooper or SS-Man armed with his 98k rifle during a training exercise.

A trainer can be seen here teaching mortar teams in the art of using the mortar during an enemy contact. The mortar being used in training is an 8cm sGrW 34. Note how all the crew duck for cover to avoid the back-blast of the projectile as it leaves the gun tube. Standard practice is for two of the ammunition-handlers or loaders to hold the tripod in order to keep it steady and accurate when firing. *(NA)*

An officer lectures his recruits during training in the summer of 1941. Due to many of the volunteers being nationalistic, their trainers often gave the men in-depth indoctrination in SS philosophy and racial superiority. These ideological teachings were aimed at producing men who ardently believed in the new Aryan order. They had to listen regularly to their trainer lecturing them about anti-Semitism. All the recruits were indoctrinated into an almost fanatical determination to serve the SS with blind allegiance. *(NA)*

During a training exercise the men are seen loading a shell into the ordnance in preparation for firing. *(NA)*

Two photographs taken during what appears to be a passing-out ceremony and the legion's standard is being carried displaying the *Frikorps Danmark* insignia.

FRIKORPS
DANMARK

A series of photographs showing Danish recruits listening to their commander during training while in formation on the barracks training grounds. While undertaking military manoeuvres the recruits often simulated as closely as possible real combat conditions using live ammunition. They were told about the tactics used by the Russian infantry and due to this, the training could be gruelling and aggressive. *(NA)*

Four photographs taken in sequence showing a formal ceremony at the training grounds in Hamburg. The images show commanding officers saluting the soldiers in a formation on parade including regimental bandsmen and trumpeters, and a speech by one of the legion's commanders on a podium to his men. *(NA)*

Seven photographs taken in sequence showing *SS-Reichsführer* Heinrich Himmler visiting the *Frikorps Danmark*. Himmler had been quite insistent about getting the legion commanders and trainers to teach the men about enemies of the state, coupled with an in-depth indoctrination into SS philosophy and their racial superiority. By continually drilling the recruits he believed it would ferment hatred and violence, especially against their arch enemy, the Russians. What Himmler did not understand was that the soldiers were militarily ill-equipped and undertrained. Yet, despite this, he thought that due to fanatical determination and blind allegiance they would succeed on the Eastern Front. *(NA)*

Two photographs taken in sequence showing a soldier on patrol duties on a typical Russian road. *(NA)*

The first of three photographs showing a PaK crew along a road during a defensive operation with their PaK 40. By the middle of the war this weapon formed the backbone of German anti-tank guns. However, although it was towed to the front, crews were not able to manhandle it properly due to its weight, especially on boggy ground. *(NA)*

A soldier on guard duty overlooking a static position. *(NA)*

Two photographs: the first showing a motorcycle combination moving along a road passing a column of stationary Volkswagen Kübelwagens, the second showing a stationary Kübelwagen parked behind a transport vehicle where local Croatian civilians were being rounded up. This unit was part of *Panzergrenadier* Regiment 24. It was sent to Croatia in September 1943 for training, where it was also used to fight partisans. *(NA)*

TISKARA

Light MG 42 machine-gunners during a pause at the front. The MG 42 proved its capabilities in both offensive and defensive actions. Its dependability was second to none and every unit of the Waffen-SS and German army was equipped with this weapon. *(NA)*

A series of images showing *Sturmgeschütz* IIIs during operations. These assault guns belonging to *Sturmgeschütz-Abteilung* 11 were part of the 11th *SS Volunteer Panzergrenadier-Division Nordland. SS-Panzergrenadier-Regiment* 24 *Danmark* supported *Nordland*. The Danish regiment was first deployed in partisan combat in Hrastovica, Sisak, Glina and Petrinja in Yugoslavia. By the end of 1943 the regiment was moved to the Eastern Front near Leningrad along with *Nordland* and *Sturmgeschütz-Abteilung* 11. *(NA)*

Chapter Four

The Last Battles of the Europeans

The resistance of Germany's once mighty armies was now collapsing amid the ruins of the Reich. Most of the so-called crack Waffen-SS divisions were still embroiled in heavy fighting in Hungary and were unable to be released in order to plug huge gaps on the German front lines in the East. This left the northern and central sectors of the Eastern Front to east and west for the European SS volunteers to defend.

Most of the German front was now held on the western bank of the Oder. In the north, the ancient city of Stettin, capital of Pomerania, and in the south the town of Kustrin were both vital holding-points against the main Russian objective of the war, Berlin.

As the great Red Army drive gathered momentum, more towns and villages fell to the onrushing forces. Suicidal opposition from a few SS and Wehrmacht strongpoints bypassed in earlier attacks reduced buildings to blasted rubble. Everywhere it seemed the Germans and their European SS counterparts were being constantly forced to retreat. Many isolated units spent hours or even days fighting a bloody defence, with a number of them deciding that their fate would be met out on the battlefield. To them they would rather bleed fighting on the grasslands of Eastern Europe than surrender and be at the mercy of a Russian soldier.

By early April the Russians prepared to push forward on the River Oder. Here along the Oder and Neisse troops waited for the front to become engulfed by the greatest concentration of firepower ever amassed by the Russians. General Zhukov's 1st Belorussian Front and General Konev's 1st Ukrainian Front were preparing to attack German forces defending positions east of Berlin. For the attack the Red Army mustered some 2.5 million men divided into four armies. They were supported by 41,600 guns and heavy mortars as well as 6,250 tanks and self-propelled guns.

The final battle before Berlin began at dawn on 16 April 1945, just 38 miles east of the German capital along the swollen River Oder. Over the course of the next three days the constant fighting saw thousands of German soldiers perish. Despite their attempts to blunt the Red Army, the road to Berlin was wrenched wide open. At this crucial moment a number of top-quality SS soldiers had been gathered in the recently-established 11th Panzer Army under the command of *SS-Obergruppenführer* Felix Steiner. The 11th Panzer Army had been given the task of launching an offensive designed to dislocate the threatened enemy advance on Berlin, but had been halted against massive attacks. When the final push on Berlin began on 16 April, the 11th Panzer Army retained only three reliable divisions. One of these, the 18th Panzergrenadier Division, was transferred from east of Berlin. A few days later the 11th *SS.Panzergrenadier-Division Nordland* was rushed to Berlin and the SS Brigade *Nederland* which was split into two *Kampfgruppen* was sent out of the capital to help stem the Russian advance.

Inside the ruined city, part of the 15th *Waffengrenadier-Division der SS* from Latvia was ordered to take up defensive positions together with the Belgian *Langemarck* and *Wallonien* divisions and the remaining volunteers of the French *Charlemagne* Division. All these Waffen-SS troops were to take part in the last apocalyptic struggle to save the Reich capital from the clutches of the Red Army.

By 25 April Berlin was completely surrounded and the next day some 500,000 Soviet troops bulldozed their way through the city. Beneath the Reich Chancellery building, which had now become Hitler's home and headquarters, the Führer was determined to save the crumbling capital and had already ordered remnants of *SS-Obergruppenführer* Felix Steiner's 11th Panzer Army to attack immediately from their positions in the Eberswalde, then to drive south, cutting off the Russian assault on Berlin. On Hitler's map the plan looked brilliant, but it was impossible to gather forces to make Steiner's *SS-Kampfgruppe* even remotely operational. The city was doomed. On 27 April, remnants of *Nordland* with what was left of *Danmark* were pushed back into the central government district of the city where they took up defence.

For the next week the battle for Berlin raged with a mixture of European Waffen-SS seen fighting bitterly with members of the *Hitlerjugend*, *Volkssturm*, Luftwaffe and Wehrmacht troops. Even as the last hours were fought out in the fiery cauldron of Berlin, SS units, lacking all provisions including many types of weapons, still tried to halt or stem Russian assaults. With all hopes of saving Berlin lost, a number of small groups from *Nordland* managed to escape the impending slaughter and reach the Americans at the Elbe's west bank, but the majority were not successful. Most were killed in the fighting or taken prisoner after they surrendered to Soviet troops.

Epilogue

By the spring of 1945, the bulk of the premier Waffen-SS divisions were carrying out a fighting withdrawal through Hungary and Austria, while on the receding Eastern Front those SS units still in action were principally European volunteer units. Even by this late stage of the war the level of determination and courage shown by both first- and second-rate SS combat formations was quite exceptional, considering that many soldiers were totally aware there was no prospect of victory. However, in the closing days of the war most Waffen-SS soldiers were determined to withdraw west and surrender to the Anglo-American forces rather than the Red Army. Few of them harboured any illusions as to the kind of treatment they would receive from the Russians. It was for this reason that the divisions of the once-vaunted SS decided to accept their fate in the West.

While most of the remaining premier Waffen-SS divisions were captured, many of the foreign volunteers did not survive on the battlefields of Eastern Europe. The *Wiking* Division, with its predominantly Western European troops, was annihilated while fighting outside Vienna. *Nordland* was decimated during the Battle of Berlin. *Nederland* was smashed to pieces during the last stages of the Battle of Berlin, and the remnants of the *Langemarck* and *Wallonien* divisions were also totally destroyed during the battle for the Reich capital.

In early May 1945, the SS European Legions were all but destroyed, and those elements that had survived the last battles fell into enemy hands. One *Kampfgruppe* of the *Nederland* Brigade broke out to the west, surrendering to the US Army, and the other *Kampfgruppe* was pushed south by the Soviet offensive into the area around Halbe. The remnants of the unit were absorbed into *Kampfgruppe Vieweger* of the 15th Waffen Grenadier Division of the SS (1st Latvian). The unit was destroyed in the Battle of the Halbe Pocket.

Appendix I

Insignia

Flemish Legion

Langemarck

Wallonien

Nederland

Landstorm Nederland

Free Corps Denmark

Nordland

Appendix II

Order of Battle

SS-Freiwilligen Legion Flandern (Flemish Legion)

Commandant: *SS-Obersturmbannführer* Michael Lippert

Order of Battle

1. Infantry (*Schütz*) Company
2. Infantry (*Schütz*) Company
3. Infantry (*Schütz*) Company
4. (*Schwere*) Company
5. (PaK) Company

Each *Schütz* (Rifle) Company had three rifle platoons and a heavy weapons platoon each comprising heavy MGs and 5cm mortars. The 4th Heavy Company comprised three platoons, each of heavy MGs and an 8cm mortar platoon. The 5th PaK Company had two PaK platoons each with 3 × 3.7cm guns and one 8cm mortar platoon.

27th SS Volunteer Division *Langemarck*

Commanders

SS-Sturmbannführer Michael Lippert (24 September 1941–2 April 1942)
SS-Obersturmbannführer Hans Albert von Lettow-Vorbeck (2 April–June 1942)
SS-Hauptsturmführer Hallmann (June 1942)
SS-Obersturmbannführer Josef Fitzthum (20 June–11 July 1942)
SS-Sturmbannführer Conrad Schellong (11 July 1942–October 1944)
SS-Oberführer Thomas Müller (October 1944–2 May 1945)

Order of Battle

6.SS Volunteer Sturmbrigade Langemarck (July 1943)

Brigade HQ

I Battalion
- 1. Company
- 2. Company
- 3. Company
- 4. (MG) Company

II Battalion
- 5. Infantry (*Schütz*) Company
- 6. *Panzerjäger* Company
- 7. *Sturmgeschütz* Company
- 8. Flak Company
- 9. Flak Company
- 10. March Company

I *Kolonne*

27th SS Volunteer Grenadier Division *Langemarck*

SS-Panzergrenadier Regiment 66
SS-Panzergrenadier Regiment 67
SS-Panzergrenadier Regiment 68
SS-Artillery Regiment 27
SS-Panzerjäger Battalion 27
SS-Signals Battalion 27
SS-Pionier Battalion 27
SS-Div.Versorgungs Regiment 27
SS-Reserve Battalion 27
SS-Medical Battalion 27
Verwaltungs Company
Propaganda Company
Kampfgruppe Schellong

28th SS Volunteer Grenadier Division *Wallonien*

Commanders

Captain Commandant Georges Jacobs (August 1941–January 1942)
Hauptmann B.E.M. Pierre Pauly (January–March 1942)
Hauptmann George Tchekhoff (March–April 1942)
SS-Sturmbannführer Lucien Lippert (April 1942–13 February 1944)
SS-Sturmbannführer Léon Degrelle as political leader of the unit
SS-Oberführer Karl Burk (21 June–18 September 1944)
SS-Standartenführer Léon Degrelle (18 September 1944–8 May 1945)

Order of Battle

SS Volunteer *Sturmbrigade Wallonien*
Brigade HQ
I Battalion
  Company
  Company
  Company
  Company
II Battalion
  Company
  Company
  Company
  Company
Artillery Battalion
I *StuG* Battery
II *StuG* Battery
War Reporter Platoon
Flak Battery (8.8cm)
Flak Battery (2.2cm)
Panzerjäger Company
Signal Company
1 Reserve Company
2 Reserve Company
I *Kolonne*

28.SS Volunteer Grenadier Division *Wallonien*

SS *Panzergrenadier* Regiment 69
I./SS-Panzergrenadier Regiment 69
II./SS-Panzergrenadier Regiment 69
SS-Panzergrenadier Regiment 70
I./SS-Panzergrenadier Regiment 70
SS-Artillery Regiment 28
SS-Panzerjäger Battalion 28
SS-Reconnaissance Battalion 28
SS-Signal Battalion 28
SS-Pionier Battalion 28
SS-Supply Company 28
SS-Flak Company 28

SS-Administration Company 28
SS-Medical Company 28
SS-Veterinarian Company 28
SS-Reserve Battalion 28
SS-Storm Battalion 28
Kampfgruppe Capelle

23rd SS Volunteer *Panzergrenadier* Division *Nederland*

Commanders

SS-Sturmbannführer Herbert Garthe (November 1941–February 1942)
SS-Oberführer Otto Reich (February–1 April 1942)
SS-Obersturmbannführer Arved Theuermann (1 April 1942–)
SS-Standartenführer Josef Fitzthum
SS-Brigadeführer Jürgen Wagner (20 April 1944–1 May 1945)

Order of Battle

SS Volunteer Legion *Nederland*
I Battalion
- 1. Company
- 2. Company
- 3. Company
- 4. Company

II Battalion
- 5. Company
- 6. Company
- 7. Company
- 8. Company

III Battalion
- 9. Company
- 10. Company
- 11. Company
- 12. Company
- 13. Artillery Company
- 14. *Panzerjäger* Company

4th SS Volunteer *Panzergrenadier-Brigade Nederland*
SS Volunteer *Panzergrenadier Regiment 48 General Seyffardt*
SS Volunteer *Panzergrenadier Regiment 49 de Ruyter*
SS Artillery Regiment 54
SS Signals Battalion 54
SS *Panzerjäger* Battalion 54
SS *Pionier* Battalion 54

34th SS Volunteer Grenadier Division *Landstorm Nederland*

Commanders

SS-Oberführer Viktor Knapp (11 May 1943–1 April 1944)
SS-Obersturmbannführer Deurheit (1 April–5 November 1944)
SS-Standartenführer Martin Kohlroser (5 November 1944–8 May 1945)

Order of Battle

34th SS Volunteer Grenadier Division *Landstorm Nederland*
Division HQ
SS *Feldersatz* Battalion 60
Grenadier-Regiment 1
SS Volunteer Grenadier Regiment 83 (3rd Dutch)

SS Volunteer Grenadier Regiment 84 (4th Dutch)
SS Artillery Regiment 60
SS *Panzerjäger* Battalion 60
SS *Pionier* Company 60
SS Signals Company 60
SS Veterinary Company 60
SS Field Post Department 60
SS Medical Company 60

11th SS Volunteer *Panzergrenadier* Division *Nordland*

Order of Battle

SS-Panzergrenadier Regiment 23 *Norge*
SS-Panzergrenadier Regiment 24 *Danmark*
SS-Panzer Battalion 11 *Hermann von Salza*
SS-Panzer Artilleree Regiment 11
SS-Panzer Reconnaissance Battalion 11
SS-Sturmgeschütz Battalion 11
SS-Panzerjäger Battalion 11
SS-Signals Battalion 11
SS-Pionier Battalion 11
SS-Nachrichtung Abteilung Truppen 11
SS-Supply Troop 11
SS-Repair Battalion 11
SS-Wirtschafts Battalion 11
SS-War Reporter Platoon 11
SS-Feldgendarmerie Troop 11
SS-Reserve Battalion 11
SS-Bewährungs Company 11
SS-Medical Battalion 11
SS-Werfer Battalion 521

Notes

Notes

Notes

Notes

Notes

Notes